A Taste of culture

Foods of Afghanistan

Barbara Sheen

KIDHAVEN PRESS
A part of Gale, Cengage Learning

GALE
CENGAGE Learning™

Detroit • New York • San Francisco • New Haven, Conn • Waterville, Maine • London

© 2011 Gale, Cengage Learning

LIBRARY OF CONGRESS CATALOGING-IN-PUBLICATION DATA

Sheen, Barbara.
 Foods of Afghanistan / by Barbara Sheen.
     p. cm. -- (A taste of culture)
 Includes bibliographical references and index.
 ISBN 978-0-7377-5420-9 (hardcover)
 1. Cooking, Afghan--Juvenile literature. 2. Afghanistan--Social life and customs. 3. Cookbooks. I. Title. II. Series.
  TX724.5.A3S55 2011
  641.59581--dc22

                                                                            2010043805

Kidhaven Press
27500 Drake Rd.
Farmington Hills MI 48331

ISBN-13: 978-0-7377-5420-9
ISBN-10: 0-7377-5420-6

Printed in the United States of America
1 2 3 4 5 6 7 15 14 13 12 11

Printed by Bang Printing, Brainerd, MN, 1st Ptg., 03/2011

Contents

A Cultural Connection

Afghanistan is a mountainous country in central Asia with a turbulent history. Since ancient times, Afghanistan has withstood repeated invasions by foreign nations wanting to establish a stronghold among Europe, the Middle East, and Asia. In addition, the population of Afghanistan is made up of more than twenty different ethnic groups that sometimes feud with each other.

Even in the hardest of times, the Afghan people have clung to their culture and traditions. The food they eat is part of this. Afghans are proud of their cooking. Most use recipes that have been passed down for generations. These recipes rely on grains, spices, yogurt,

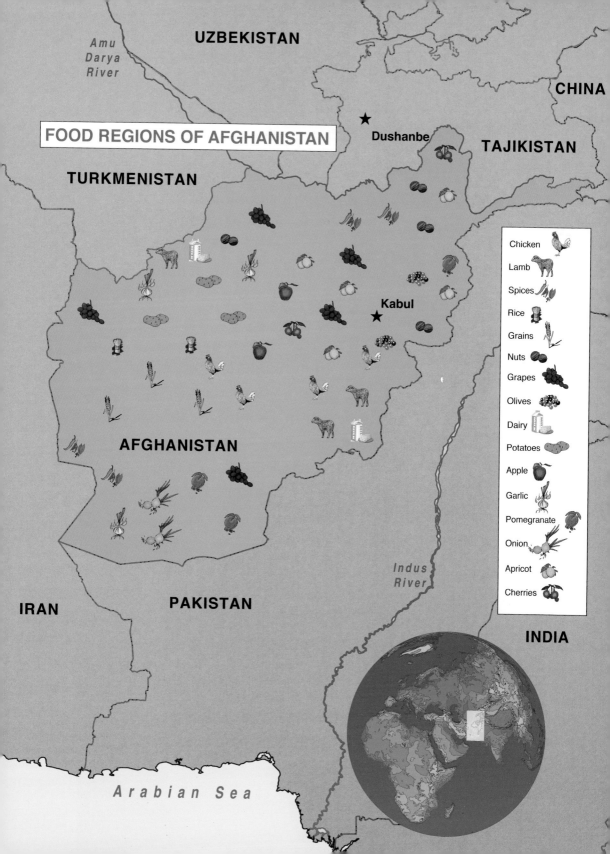

FOOD REGIONS OF AFGHANISTAN

Amu
Darya
River

UZBEKISTAN

CHINA

★ Dushanbe

TAJIKISTAN

TURKMENISTAN

★ Kabul

AFGHANISTAN

Indus
River

IRAN

PAKISTAN

INDIA

Arabian Sea

Chicken	
Lamb	
Spices	
Rice	
Grains	
Nuts	
Grapes	
Olives	
Dairy	
Potatoes	
Apple	
Garlic	
Pomegranate	
Onion	
Apricot	
Cherries	

and dried fruits and nuts. These ingredients connect Afghanistan's different ethnic groups. They are the foundation of Afghan meals and an important part of Afghan life.

Important Grains

Wheat is a mainstay of Afghan cooking. It is used to make dumplings, noodles, pastries, and bread. Bread, in particular, is vital to Afghan life. **Naan** (nahn), the word for bread in **Dari**, one of two official languages of Afghanistan, also means food. It is served fresh and hot with every meal.

Naan is made with whole wheat flour and a small lump of sourdough, which is a dough made with harmless bacteria that gives it a tart flavor. The bread is baked in a **tandoor** (tahn-DOOR). A tandoor is a

A flat bread called naan, made from whole wheat and sourdough, is a staple of the diet of the Afghan people.

beehive-shaped clay oven that is heated with charcoal to reach temperatures as high as 850°F (450°C). The high heat allows the bread, which is placed inside the tandoor with a long paddle, to bake quickly.

Most Afghan families do not own a tandoor. Instead, villagers often take their dough to a village bakery that has a tandoor. Author Helen Saberi recalls, "My servant used to prepare the dough first thing in the morning … and carry … [the dough balls] on her head balanced on a large tray made from woven straw to the nanwaee (tandoor bakery). … She would collect the bread later on, usually in time for lunch."[1]

Eating in Afghanistan

Traditionally, Afghans eat around large colorful cloth or straw mats spread on the floor over beautiful rugs that Afghanistan is famous for. Diners sit cross-legged on large cushions placed around the cloth. Food is served on platters from which everyone shares. Utensils are not typically used. Instead, diners scoop up food with pieces of bread.

Afghans eat with their right hand. The left hand, which is used for personal hygiene, is never used for eating. Before eating, a pitcher of water is brought out. The water is poured on the diners' hands to clean them.

Families eat together. But if guests are present, due to cultural reasons or religious restrictions, the women and men eat separately. And, although the women typically prepare the food, a male child will serve the male diners.

With its soft, rippled surface and golden crust, naan looks something like a small pizza without the toppings. It has a soft texture, a slightly sour flavor, and an earthy aroma. Afghans eat it without butter or other toppings. And, since Afghans do not usually use utensils, they use the bread to sop up soup and pick up food.

Rice

Rice is another important grain. It has been the centerpiece of Afghan meals since ancient **Silk Road** travelers brought it to Afghanistan from India. Afghan

Basmati rice, known as chalau, is a key part of many meals served in Afghan homes.

cooks make many different rice dishes. Most start with **chalau** (chahl-OW), a fluffy mound of snow-white basmati (bahs-MAH-tee) rice, a type of long-grain rice

The Silk Road

The Silk Road is the name given to a network of trails that connected ancient civilizations in Asia to those in the Middle East, Europe, and North Africa. The Silk Road extended over 4,000 miles (6,437km). The southern route of the Silk Road passed through Afghanistan.

The Silk Road allowed ancient people to trade with each other. Silk, carried by caravans from China to Rome, was one of the most important products traded and gave the road its name. But silk was not the only thing that was exchanged. Gold, glass, and precious metals were carried to China. Jewels and spices were carried from India to the west. More importantly, the interaction of the travelers along the road allowed the exchange of cultures among ancient people, including religion, foods, and technology.

A camel caravan is depicted traveling along the Silk Road, along which traders from Asia, North Africa, and Europe trekked to bring their goods to other parts of the ancient world.

with a flowery fragrance. Chalau is usually topped with vegetables, meat, and delicious sauces.

Afghan cooks are very particular about their rice. Each grain must be dry, light, and fluffy. Making a perfect bowl of chalau is not easy. First, cooks soak the rice in water to clean it and get rid of excess starch. Then they parboil, or partially boil, it. Next, they drain off the cooking water and add more water or meat juices, oil, salt, and spices. Finally the rice is baked. As it bakes, a crisp, golden crust known as tie daygi (tah DEE-gee) forms at the bottom of the pan. It is considered a special treat that is sliced like a pie and served separately.

Since many Afghans do not own ovens, they "bake" the rice in a large pot over a charcoal fire. Or, they exclude this step, and finish cooking the rice on a stovetop.

The rice is served on a big platter placed in the center of the eating surface. The rice must be snow white, soft, fluffy, fragrant, and never sticky. According to Humaira Ghilzai and Katie Morford, the authors of Afghan Cooking Unveiled, a website dedicated to Afghan food and culture, "Nothing is more important to the Afghan table than the rice. An Afghan woman's reputation as a good cook can hinge solely on how well she prepares rice."[2]

Spices

Like rice, spices were introduced into Afghanistan thousands of years ago by Silk Road traders. Afghan cooks have been using them to color, flavor, and per-

A man sells spices in a market in Kabul, Afghanistan. Cardamom, cumin, cloves, mint, and ginger are among the spices commonly used by Afghan cooks.

fume their food ever since. Some of these spices, such as cinnamon, mint, cloves, pepper, and ginger, are familiar to North Americans, while others are less so. Cardamom is a sweet aromatic spice similar to ginger. Afghan cooks add it to rice, tea, and desserts. Cumin is another. It has a slightly bitter taste and a musky scent, which complements rice and meat dishes.

Afghans buy spices whole and grind them into a powder in a stone dish, known as a mortar, with a small, wooden club-like tool called a pestle. Spices may be ground and used individually, or they may be blended together to make **char masala** (chahr mah-SAH-lah), a popular spice mix made of cumin, cloves, cinnamon, and cardamom. Char masala gives Afghan dishes a sweet-savory taste and a mouthwatering aroma, without making the dishes overly hot and spicy.

Yogurt

Yogurt, or **mast** (mahst), as it is known in Afghanistan, is another traditional part of the Afghan people's diet. Mast is thicker and richer than American yogurt. It has a cool, creamy, sour taste that is a perfect counterbalance to the sweet, warming spices that are vital to Afghan cooking. Also, yogurt is loaded with nutrients and contains harmless bacteria that take up space in a person's digestive tract. Because of this, it helps promote good health.

Afghans use mast in dozens of ways. They add it to stews and soups. They dip vegetables and naan in it. They turn it into sauces. They marinate meat in it. They mix it with club soda, mint, and salt to make a refreshing

Freshly made yogurt, known as mast, can be served on its own or used as an ingredient for a larger meal.

Yogurt Sauce

Afghans use this sauce on vegetables, meat, and noodles. It also makes a good dip for pita bread, and can be poured over salad.

Ingredients
1 cup plain yogurt (Greek yogurt, if available)
1 teaspoon minced garlic
½ teaspoon dried mint leaves, minced
salt and pepper to taste

Instructions
1. Combine all the ingredients in a small bowl. Mix well.
2. Serve immediately or cover and chill in the refrigerator.
Makes 1 cup.

drink called doogh (doog). They eat it plain. And, since many Afghans do not own refrigerators, they preserve mast by straining, salting, and drying it so that it forms hard balls called quroot (kuh-ROOT), which can be kept for long periods without spoiling. Mast, according to Morford, "always has a presence at the table whether poured over, stirred into, or resting atop a cooked dish, or served plain, usually spiked with dried garlic and a touch of salt."[3]

Nuts and Dried Fruit

Nuts and dried fruit are also traditional elements of Afghan cooking. Afghans like combining sweet and savory flavors. Adding walnuts, almonds, pistachios, raisins,

A shop in a Kabul market offers a variety of dried fruits and nuts, which are traditional ingredients in Afghan cooking.

prunes, and dried apricots to stews and sauces give these dishes the sweet and savory taste that Afghans love. Dried fruit and nuts are featured in Afghan snacks and desserts. Kishmash paneer (KEESH-mash PAH-neer), soft, white cheese served with raisins is a popular treat in Afghanistan. Raisins are so popular that many Afghan homes have a special room where grapes are hung to dry on long poles that line the walls. Openings in the walls allow outside air to circulate through the grapes, turning them into raisins.

Afghan raisins come in many sizes and shapes. They may be plump, shriveled, big, small, black, red, green, or yellow. In fact, until about 40 years ago, when war and political uncertainty hampered raisin production

Doogh

Afghans enjoy this refreshing drink on hot summer days. It is easy to make.

Ingredients
3 cups cold water or club soda
1 cup plain yogurt
pinch of salt
1 tablespoon finely chopped fresh mint

Instructions
1. Put the water, yogurt, and salt into a blender and mix well.
2. Fill four glasses with the mixture. Top with mint. Add ice cubes to cool.

Serves 4.

in Afghanistan, the country was the world's leading producer of raisins.

But, no matter the political conditions in Afghanistan, the Afghan people have always taken pride in their cooking. Their use of grains, spices, yogurt, and dried fruit and nuts remains constant. These ingredients help connect the Afghan people with their culture. They are the centerpieces of recipes that Afghan cooks have proudly passed down for generations.

An Honored Tradition

Hospitality is an honored tradition in Afghanistan. Guests are always welcomed into Afghan homes where they are offered the best foods, even if that means the hosts do not get that food for themselves. For a guest to leave an Afghan home hungry is unthinkable. According to writer Paul Kvinta who visited Afghanistan for *National Geographic Adventure*, "The … thing that made an impression is the [Afghans'] incredible hospitality. It's an exalted cultural value in Afghanistan. It is impossible to visit or interview anyone without an amazing spread of food and drink being laid out before me."[4] Favorite dishes such as **palau** (pahl-OW), **korma** (KOR-mah), **mantu** (MAHN-too), and **ashak** (AH-shahk) are likely to be on the menu.

Muslim Dietary Rules

Most Afghans are Muslims. They follow dietary rules set down by the Koran, their holy book. Acceptable food is said to be halal, which means lawful. Unacceptable foods are said to be haram, or forbidden.

Haram foods include pork and pork products such as gelatin, animal blood, the meat of carnivores such as dogs, wolves, rats, lions, and bears, birds of prey like eagles, and land animals without external ears like snakes. Meat of animals offered in religious sacrifice, killed by other animals, by beating or strangulation, or by an accident, also is not permitted. Alcoholic beverages are forbidden, as well.

To be halal, animals must be slaughtered in a way that causes it the least pain. This involves cutting the major arteries in the animal's throat, which causes all the blood to drain out of its body.

Halal goat meat hangs in a butcher shop in Kabul, Afghanistan. For meat to be considered halal, a butcher must slaughter the animal according to specific rules.

Palau

Afghan meals are communal events. Typically, large platters piled with different entrées are placed in the center of the eating surface for everyone to share. Palau is likely to be among these dishes. It consists of meat, vegetables, and sometimes fruit arranged in alternating layers with rice. The dish originated in Persia (now Iran) and was brought to Afghanistan by Persian invaders around A.D. 550.

Afghan cooks make dozens of different types of palau. "The number of ways palau can be cooked,"

Qabili palau, known as Afghanistan's national dish, is made of rice, lamb or chicken, carrots, onions, raisins, and spices.

says author Nafisa Sekandari, "depends on the chef's imagination."[5]

Most contain lamb, beef, or chicken, but not pork. This is because most Afghans are Muslims, followers of the Islam religion, many of whom follow strict dietary rules that forbid the eating of pork. Different vegetables, dried fruits, and nuts are also featured. For instance, pale green sabzi palau (SAHB-zee pahl-OW), features spinach, onions, and lamb, while sweetly scented norinj palau (nor-EENJ pahl-OW) contains chicken, orange peels, almonds, pistachio nuts, and onions.

Qabili palau (kah-BEE-lee pahl-OW) is another favorite. It is Afghanistan's national dish. Making this colorful mixture of rice, lamb or chicken, spices, shredded carrots, onions, and raisins requires many steps. First, cooks brown the meat and onions in plenty of oil; then they simmer the mixture in water until the meat is as soft as butter. The tender meat is removed from the pan, and the meat juices are saved for later. Next, cooks brown the raisins and carrots with brown sugar. They cook the rice, seasoned with char masala, in the meat juices. Finally, they layer half the rice on the bottom of a casserole. They top it with the meat, followed by another layer of rice. The whole thing is crowned with the carrots and raisins and baked like chalau. Right before the dish is served, a drop of rosewater, a liquid made with distilled water and rose petals, is sprinkled on top. The finished dish is beautiful, moist, and fragrant, tasting sweet and spicy and smelling like an exotic garden.

Korma

Korma is another fragrant, tasty Afghan dish. Whether served at family meals or as a way to honor guests, this thin stew is a part of almost every Afghan meal.

Korma originated in India and was brought to Afghanistan by Silk Road travelers. Afghan cooks adapted the dish to their taste by making it less hot and spicy than Indian korma.

There are probably as many varieties of korma as there are cooks in Afghanistan. Most Afghan kormas contain meat, although meatless kormas are not uncommon. All kormas start with plenty of fried onions, which Afghans use in almost everything. The onions thicken the korma and add a bitter-sweet flavor. Chunks of lamb, beef, or chicken   are

Korma, a thin stew usually served over rice, can include a variety of meats, vegetables, fruits, and spices.

Chicken Korma

Korma is not difficult to make. Cauliflower or spinach can be substituted for chicken.

Ingredients
1 onion, chopped
1 cooked chicken, bones removed, cut into chunks
¼ cup olive oil
1 tablespoon minced garlic
1 tablespoon tomato paste
1 cup plain yogurt
1 cup water
1 teaspoon each of cumin, mint, crushed red pepper.
salt to taste

Instructions
1. Put the oil in a frying pan. Add the onions, garlic, red pepper, cumin, and mint. Fry over medium heat until the onions are soft.
2. Lower the heat. Add the chicken, water, tomato paste, and yogurt. Cover the pot. Cook on low until the sauce thickens. Salt to taste.
3. Serve over rice.
Serves 4.

added. The meat is browned quickly over high heat. Water, mashed tomatoes, spices, such as garlic, ginger, cumin, and turmeric (a slightly bitter bright-yellow spice), and a variety of fruits, vegetables, and **legumes**, such as mashed split peas or lentils, are added. The legumes give the korma a velvety texture. Once all the ingredients are in the cooking pot, the korma is cooked slowly until all the flavors blend together and every ingredient is buttery soft.

Anything and everything can be used in korma. Sometimes yogurt is added, which makes the stew rich and creamy and gives it a tart flavor. Some kormas contain dried apricots or prunes. While still others feature star cauliflower, mushrooms, carrots, or apples. No matter the exact ingredients, all Afghan kormas are mildly spiced and quite fragrant. They are not as heavy as American stews, but rather have the consistency of a thick sauce. This makes korma perfect for pouring over rice, which is exactly what Afghans do. Sekandari says, "The idea of a quarma [korma] appears quite foreign to Westerners, but it is the basic staple of the Afghan meal. At my house, we eat different quarmas with rice on a daily basis. You put the quarma over your rice and eat."[6]

Favorite Noodle Dishes

Besides being poured over rice, korma also tops noodle dishes. Noodles, which are called khameerbob (kah-MEER-bob) in Afghanistan, are traditional favorites, which are often prepared for honored guests. Noodles found their way to Afghanistan via Silk Road travelers coming from China. Mantu and ashak, filled noodle dishes similar to Chinese wontons or dumplings, are by far the most popular khameerbob dishes in Afghanistan.

Little stuffed dumplings known as mantu are a traditional food of the Uzbeks, one of the many ethnic groups in Afghanistan.

Mantu is a dumpling that is filled with minced lamb and onions sprinkled with cumin. It is often topped with carrot korma, tomato sauce, or yogurt flavored with mint and garlic. This tasty little package is a traditional Uzbek (UHZ-beck) dish. The Uzbeks are one of the many ethnic groups that make up Afghanistan.

Ashak is similar to mantu. It looks like large, flat ravioli. It is filled with **gandana** (gahn-DAH-na), a popular Afghan vegetable that is a member of the onion family and tastes like a sweeter, less bitter version of a green onion. Ashak is usually topped with layers of sauce.

About Afghanistan

Afghanistan is a mountainous landlocked country in south-central Asia that is about the size of Texas. It is bordered by Uzbekistan, Tajikistan, and Turkmenistan in the north, Pakistan in the south and east, and Iran in the west. The Hindu Kush mountain range covers most of the country. Afghanistan's climate is dry. There is not enough rain for crops to grow without irrigation.

Afghanistan is an Islamic Republic. It is ruled by both civil and religious laws. It is one of the poorest nations in the world. Many Afghans face shortages of fresh water, electricity, medical care, and jobs.

Most Afghans are farmers and herders. Some are nomads, people who live in tents and move from place to place seeking grazing grounds for their sheep and camels.

Pashtu and Dari are the two official languages of Afghanistan, but over 30 different languages are spoken in Afghanistan.

First comes the yogurt sauce, followed by minced meat and tomato sauce, and finally, a sprinkling of fragrant dried mint.

Making mantu and ashak is not easy. Typically, Afghan cooks make the dumplings from scratch rather than using dried or frozen noodles. This involves making dough, which must be rolled out repeatedly until it is quite thin. It also involves preparing the filling and the sauces. This takes time and effort. When everything is ready, the cook cuts the dough into squares and carefully drops a spoonful of filling in each. Then the corners of the dumplings are folded over each other, forming plump little pouches that are pinched closed, and either steamed or boiled until the dumplings are soft and fluffy and the filling is moist and tender. Because making mantu and ashak is complicated, families often get together in large groups to make the dumplings together. Katie Morford reports that her Afghan friend and fellow cook, Humairia Ghilzai, "remembers large groups of extended family gather-

Afghan Salad

Salads are usually served as a side dish in Afghanistan. They are eaten with the meal rather than before it. This is a typical Afghan salad. Cilantro can be substituted for mint.

Ingredients
2 large ripe tomatoes
¼ cucumber, peeled
1 small sweet red onion
2 tablespoons fresh mint, chopped
juice of 1 lemon
salt and pepper to taste

Instructions
1. Cut the tomatoes, onion, and cucumber into small chunks.
2. Put the vegetables and the mint in a salad bowl. Add lemon juice, salt, and pepper. Mix.
Serves 4.

ing for the sole purpose of making aushak [ashak]. The festivities would conclude with everyone sitting down together over heaping platters of dumplings."[7]

The dumplings are served on a glistening platter topped with sauce and, if there are guests present, plenty of olive oil. Oil is scarce in Afghanistan and considered quite valuable. Therefore, topping favorite foods with lots of it is a way to honor guests. With or without oil, the dumplings are always a special treat. They have a fresh, mildly spicy taste, a light, tender texture, and a mouthwatering aroma, which make both guests and family members feel special. Indeed, with moist plump dumplings, flavorful kormas, and mouthwatering palaus piled before them, any guest would feel honored. These favorite Afghan dishes are both welcoming and delicious.

Tea and Snacks

Afghans enjoy stopping at tea houses, **kebab** (kuh-BAHB) stands, street vendors' carts, and ice cream parlors for a snack.

Tea

Tea, or chai (chy) as it is called in Afghanistan, is a favorite Afghan treat. Afghans sip it throughout the day. Tea breaks are a common practice in Afghan offices, and the drink is always served during business meetings. Even shopkeepers offer tea to their customers.

In Afghanistan sharing tea is a way to share conversation and friendship, which is why the hot drink is always served to guests. To not do so is unacceptable. In fact, unless guests put their hand over their teacup

Afghan men gather at a chaikhana, or tea shop, to relax and visit.

and say "bus" (buhs) the Dari word for enough, they will be served cup after cup. While visiting Afghanistan, British television personality Konnie Huq noted, "Everywhere I went people would insist that I drink green tea with them and made me feel that we'd been friends for years."[8]

Silk Road traders brought tea to Afghanistan from China. Over time, it became the Afghan people's favorite beverage. Most Afghan towns have at least one chaikhana (chy-KHAN-ah) or tea house, where Afghan men go to relax, visit, play chess, and drink strong hot tea. Afghan women prefer to share tea with each other

Cultural Differences

Religious laws and cultural differences make the way males and females interact in Afghanistan different than in North America. Afghan men and women who are not related to each other are kept separate. They do not speak to each other, socialize with each other, or touch each other, not even to shake hands. At social events, men and women celebrate in separate rooms.

When Afghan women go outside, they dress modestly and wear a head scarf in order to protect themselves from unwanted male attention, which is considered insulting. Many Afghan women wear a chadri, a loose-fitting garment that covers the body from head to foot, with slits for the eyes.

Afghan children also interact differently. After age six, unrelated boys and girls do not play together. Boys and girls attend separate schools. Afghan teens do not date. Marriages are arranged by parents.

A woman shops at a market wearing a chadri, a loose-fitting garment that many Afghan women wear when out in public.

in their homes.

Chaikhanas are not fancy places. They are usually small, noisy establishments where customers sit on raised platforms covered with carpet. Saberi explains:

> Each customer has his own small teapot plus a small bowl for the dregs [tea leaves]. When the tea is served, the customer rinses out his glass or bowl with the hot tea and pours this into the dregs bowl. Then he puts sugar, usually quite a lot, into his glass and adds fresh hot tea. There are no chairs in a chaikhana so people sit around cross-legged, on rugs and carpets on a specially constructed, raised platform. The walls are also covered with carpets and pictures and there is usually popular Afghan or Indian music playing in the background, which can be quite loud.[9]

Water for the tea is heated in a Russian kettle known as a samovar (SAM-uh-var). It is an urn-like device with a spigot in front that is specially designed to heat and dispense water. The hot water is poured into a teapot along with a heaping spoonful of tea per person, plus one for the pot. A sprinkle of cardamom is also added. It gives the tea a pleasant, spicy taste and a delicate floral scent. Then, the tea is left to steep until it is quite strong.

Afghans drink both green and black tea, with green

tea being the more popular choice. Each customer in a chaikhana is served an individual pot of tea. Customers drink the tea from a clear glass or a bowl-like cup. Since neither has a handle, the glass or cup is hot to the touch. This makes holding them without getting burned

Spiced Chickpeas

Spiced chickpeas are often served with tea. They are a healthy and popular snack in Afghanistan. Different spice blends can be used for a variety of flavors. Spiced chickpeas can be eaten hot or cool.

Ingredients
1 can (16 oz.) chickpeas
2 tablespoons olive oil
1 tablespoon garlic powder
1 tablespoon chili powder
1 tablespoon cumin
1 teaspoon salt

Instructions
1. Preheat oven to 375°F.
2. Drain the chickpeas in a colander. Wash them with cold water until no white foam appears. Drain the chickpeas and pat them dry. Put them in a bowl.
3. Mix the spices and oil together. Pour the mixture over the chickpeas. Mix well.
4. Spray a cookie sheet with nonstick spray. Put the chickpeas on the sheet in one layer. Bake until the chickpeas are browned, around 40–50 minutes.
5. Makes two cups.
Serves 2–4.

difficult. Afghans do not add milk or cream to their tea. But they do like sugar. Often Afghans add sugar to their first cup of tea then drink another cup without it. Some Afghans put a lump of sugar or a piece of hard candy on their tongues and sip the tea through it.

Little bowls of bite-size snacks such as almonds, walnuts, pistachio nuts, raisins, figs, dried apricots, and chickpeas almost always accompany tea.

Kebabs

Kebabs are another popular snack. Although most North Americans think of kebabs as grilled meat threaded through skewers and cooked over a charcoal fire, in Afghanistan kebabs refer to any meat that is grilled, fried,

Kebabs made from marinated, grilled lamb or other meats are usually served with hot naan as a snack or a meal.

baked, or roasted. Grilled skewered kebabs, however, are far and away the most popular.

Afghans have been eating meat cooked on a stick for centuries. Ancient shepherds roasted chunks of lamb on twigs over an open fire as they tended their flocks. Today, street stands manned by vendors known as kebabis [kuh-BAHB-ees] can be found throughout Afghanistan. The mouthwatering aroma of sizzling meat cooking over hot charcoal entices hungry passersby to stop for a snack.

Kebabs are usually made with lamb fillet. But lamb liver, kidney, ground lamb, beef, and chicken kebabs are also popular. All are made in the same way. First the kebabi **marinates** the meat in a tasty mix of yogurt, lemon juice, and spices. The acid in the marinating liquid makes the meat soft and tender.

When the meat is ready for cooking, the kebabi threads it onto a thin metal skewer known as a sikh (seek). Pieces of lamb fat taken from the animal's tail are placed between every slice of meat. As the meat cooks, fat from the tail pieces drips onto the meat, moistening it.

The kebabi fans the charcoals to keep the fire going and turns the sikh as the kebab cooks. When the meat is brown on the outside and juicy on the inside, it is ready to eat. The kebabi removes the meat from the sikh and sprinkles it with a spice mix made from crushed grape seeds, cumin, and red pepper. Then, he piles the meat on a platter. It is usually accompanied

Beef Kebab

Kebabs can be made on an indoor or outdoor grill or in a broiler. This recipe uses beef. Chunks of chicken or lamb can be substituted. Use metal skewers to cook the meat.

Ingredients
1 pound beef tenderloin, cut into cubes
1 tablespoon plain yogurt
1 teaspoon crushed garlic
1 tablespoon lime juice
1 teaspoon crushed red pepper
1 teaspoon chopped cilantro
1 tablespoon olive oil
salt to taste
4 slices of pita bread

Instructions
1. Mix all the ingredients except the meat in a bowl.
2. Place the meat in the mixture and refrigerate at least two hours.
3. Thread the meat onto the skewers. Grill the meat on a grill or in a broiler. When the meat browns on one side, turn the skewer over. The meat is done when it is brown on the outside and pinkish brown on the inside.
4. Remove the meat from the skewers. Serve with the bread. Serves 4.

by onions, tomatoes, and hot naan, which diners wrap around the tender chunks of juicy meat.

Afghan Hamburgers
Kebab stalls also serve up fried kebabs. **Chapli kebabs** (chah-PLEE kuh-BAHBS), which are often called

Afghan hamburgers, are a favorite. Chapli means "sandal" in Dari. This local favorite is indeed shaped like a large sandal or a flattened football. Made with ground lamb or beef mixed with dried chili, cilantro, cumin, and garlic, it is one of the spiciest dishes served in Afghanistan.

Kite Fighting

Kite fighting is a popular sport in Afghanistan. Most kite fighters make their own kites from tissue paper and bamboo. They also make their own kite line. The line is made of wire that is coated with rice glue and ground glass. The glass serves as a weapon against other kites. To protect themselves, kite fighters wrap a piece of leather around their index finger while handling the line.

When the line is ready it is attached to the kite. Excess line can be 1,000 feet (305m) long, so it is wound into a wooden drum and released during the kite fight.

When the kites are in the air, fighters try to cut their opponents' kites free of their lines. There can be up to 25 kites in the air during a fight. Kite fights can last for a few minutes or several hours.

An Afghan boy flies a kite from the top of a hill. Kite fighting is a popular sport in Afghanistan.

Before it is served, the meat is sprinkled with coriander or pomegranate seeds and a squeeze of lemon juice. Naan, of course, accompanies it. Writer Jiffer Bourguignon who ate chapli kebabs in Kabul, Afghanistan's capital, says: "The combination of spices, the slight crunch of pomegranate seeds, the tangy but not overpowering garlic, and the heat of the chiles and black pepper, it is divine."[10]

Handmade Ice Cream

Ice cream, or sheer yakh, as it is known in Afghanistan, is another divine treat. It is sold in ice cream parlors and by street vendors throughout Afghanistan. It is especially popular during Afghanistan's hot summers.

Sheer yakh is handmade and contains no chemicals or preservatives. Afghans have been making it in much the same way for thousands of years. To do so, they use a device that looks like a large metal bucket filled with ice.

A smaller bucket, which fits inside the larger one, is filled with milk, sugar, and flavorings such as vanilla,

A man scoops an ice cream treat known as sheer yakh at a restaurant in Afghanistan.

cardamom, or nuts. Ice cream makers use their hands to move the small bucket from side to side, until the ingredients become thick, frozen, and creamy.

Sheer yakh is often topped with thick cream, rosewater, crushed pistachio nuts, and crisp, sweet noodles to make an Afghan version of an ice cream sundae. National Public Radio (NPR) reporter Ivan Watson recently sampled some on a summer's day in the Afghan city of Jalalabad, "It melts fast," he noted. "But for a sweet moment offers a much needed escape from the Jalalabad heat."[11]

Snacks like handmade ice cream, sweet green tea, and juicy kebabs offer Afghans many delicious moments. The taste of these treats is irresistible.

4

Special Foods for Special Days

Afghans like to celebrate. Sharing food is an important part of every celebration. Holidays and special occasions give Afghans a chance to share special foods with family and friends.

Fasting and Feasting

Afghanistan is a Muslim nation. Most Afghan celebrations are tied to religious holy days. **Ramadan** (RAH-mah-dahn), a month-long religious holiday that falls at different times each year, is an important time of the year. During Ramadan, Muslims typically fast from dawn to dusk in an effort to purify their souls. This includes giving up all food and drink. Daily meals are limited to two: suhoor (SOO-hoor), a predawn meal

Dishes of food await a group of Afghan men who are preparing to break their sunrise-to-sunset fast during the holy month of Ramadan.

that starts the daily fast, and iftar (IF-tahr), the evening meal that breaks it.

Traditionally, Afghan families gather together for the nightly iftar meal. Friends, neighbors, and even strangers are welcomed. According to Fatima, an Afghan woman, "Ramadan is a time when people come together, and in my household having iftar with the family is the most important part of this month."[12]

The Iftar Meal

Iftar menus vary, but most meals start with dates. Dates are sweet fruits similar to figs. They can be eaten fresh or dried. This tradition started in the 7th century

Afghan Homes and Families

Afghan homes are usually made of brick plastered with mud and straw. In cities, most people live in high-rise apartment buildings. Some Afghan homes have running water and modern plumbing, but many do not. Most homes do not have a lot of furniture. Afghans prefer to sit on cushions atop beautiful rugs. They spread thin mattresses on the rugs to sleep on at night, then stack the mattresses in a corner during the day.

Many people usually live together in an Afghan home. Most Afghans live in extended family groups either in the same house or in separate homes that are clustered together. The family group usually includes grandparents, parents, and brothers with their wives and children. The women help each other with the household chores and with raising the children.

Afghan women prepare a meal in a traditional home, which usually includes many generations and extended family members.

when the Muslim prophet Muhammad broke his daily Ramadan fast with dates.

Next, Afghans eat a light appetizer before taking a break to pray. A popular choice of food is **boulani** (boo-LAH-nee). It is a fried bread stuffed with potatoes or with a vegetable called gandana, which is similar to chives. Making boulani takes a lot of time and effort, which may be why it is mainly prepared just for special occasions. To make boulani, the cook first makes the dough. Since Afghan flour often contains impurities, it must be sifted multiple times to remove the impurities and to break up clumps. Sifting flour also adds air to it, which makes the boulani light.

Once the flour is ready, water, salt, and oil are added. The cook then kneads the dough until it is smooth and shiny. Next, the cook rolls the dough out over and over

Dates, a sweet fruit similar to figs, are often eaten at the start of the iftar meal.

again in order to get it paper thin. If the dough is too thick, the boulani will be hard.

The filling is made, too. The gandana or potatoes are cooked, mashed, and spiced.

Once everything is ready, the cook cuts the dough into 6-inch (15.24cm) circles and spoons the filling onto it. Then, the dough is folded into triangles and fried in hot oil until the boulani is golden on the outside and hot and moist within.

Usually, boulani is served piping hot, right out of the frying pan. It is topped with a creamy yogurt sauce spiced with garlic and mint. The end result is fresh, light, crisp, moist, and delicious.

A Three-Day Festival

When Ramadan ends, Afghans mark the end of fasting with a three-day festival known as Eid ul-Fitr (ide uhl-FET-ter). It is celebrated with a great deal of joy and excitement. Children receive gifts of new clothes, adults exchange greeting cards, and families and friends visit each other. In fact, Afghans open their homes day and night for anyone who wants to drop in. Tea and a spread of dried fruits, spiced chickpeas, sugared almonds, nut brittle, and different types of sweets are set out for guests. **Halwa** (HAHL-wah), is usually among these sweets.

Halwa is an interesting item that is eaten throughout central Asia, India, and the Middle East. In some parts of the world, halwa is solid and crumbly. Afghan halwa is more like a rich, thick pudding. It can be

A version of halwa, a treat made with shredded carrots, milk, raisins, nuts, and cardamom, is often enjoyed by Afghans during festivities marking the end of Ramadan.

made from different grains, or sweet vegetables like beets or carrots, mixed with sugar, dried fruit, nuts, and milk. Wheat and carrot halwa are the most popular varieties in Afghanistan. Wheat halwa is traditionally served after Afghan funerals, and is known as halwa of the dead. It is also handed out to the poor on religious holidays.

Carrot halwa is associated with happy occasions like Eid ul-fitr. To make the bright orange treat, cooks slowly heat shredded carrots with milk, raisins, nuts, and cardamom. As the halwa cooks, the liquid is absorbed and the flavors and textures blend together forming a thick, sweet, soft, lightly scented dessert that is served warm with a cup of tea. According to Katie Morford, halwa is "sweet like dessert, but it's got enough carrots to qualify for a salad. ... It's unlike anything I've ever eaten before. But it's worth eating: gently flavored with cardamom and rosewater, warm, rich, and satisfying. ... It's the perfect sort of thing to share with a friend over tea. ... Homey, warm, pleasing, nourishing, wholesome."[13]

Carrot Halwa

Carrot halwa is not difficult to make, but it does take time. It can be made on a stovetop or in a slow cooker.

Ingredients
1 lb. carrots, peeled and shredded
1¼ cup milk
¼ cup cream
½ cup sugar
½ cup butter
½ cup raisins
1 teaspoon cardamom

Instructions
1. Combine all the ingredients in a large pot. Cook on low until most of the liquid has absorbed, about one hour, stirring often.
2. Serve hot or refrigerate and serve chilled. Top with chopped nuts.
Serves 4.

New Year's Treats

Nauroz (NAW-rose) is another festive holiday. This twelve-day celebration marks the start of the Afghan New Year and the first day of spring. It is one of only a few holidays in Afghanistan that is not tied to the Muslim religion. In fact, because of its nonreligious origin, the repressive government known as the Taliban banned the holiday when it ruled from 1996 until 2001.

Afghans, Iranians, and people in central Asia have been celebrating Nauroz for at least 3,000 years. Afghans cook a number of special dishes especially for Nauroz. One, **samanak** (sah-mahn-AHK), is almost as

Buzkashi

Afghans have long been known as excellent horsemen. Afghanistan's national sport, buzkashi (booz-KAH-shee) shows off this skill. Afghan men have been playing it for thousands of years.

Buzkashi is played on horseback in an open field. The object of the game is for a rider to grab the carcass of a dead goat off the ground, move it across the field past the other riders, and toss it into a circle.

The animal used in the game is beheaded, its legs are cut off at the knees, and its insides are removed. It is soaked in cold water for a day, so that it becomes hard and leathery.

Buzkashi is a rough sport. It is played at full gallop. The horses are trained to stand still should a rider be thrown. Riders crash into each other and hit each other with whips to prevent an opponent from successfully tossing the carcass into the circle.

Afghan men on horseback play buzkashi, their country's national sport.

ancient as the holiday itself.

Samanak is a sweet pudding that takes lots of preparation. The preparation starts about twenty days before Nauroz, when Afghan women plant wheat in gardening trays. The evening before Nauroz, women get together at a party also known as samanak. The party lasts all night. Guests cook the samanak while having fun visiting, feasting on favorite foods, dancing, and singing a special samanak-making song.

"The party," explains Zarmina, an Afghan woman, "is for 15 women or 40, all friends and family. Laughing, dancing, new clothes, makeup, the whole night dancing and eating … and singing. … The singing is beautiful and it is always a special time for Afghan women. … We usually do not go to sleep until 3 in the morning!"[14]

To make the samanak, the women first grind and clean the tender green wheat sprouts. They combine the wheat with flour and water in a big pot that they heat over an outdoor fire. The concoction is cooked until it becomes the consistency of yogurt. This takes about fourteen hours. The pot is never left unattended. The women take turns stirring the samanak. When it is done, they each have a bowl. But most of the samanak is reserved for the next day when it is shared with everyone in the family, both male and female.

Samanak is brown and grainy. Even though it does not contain sugar, it tastes surprisingly sweet. This is because as it cooks the young wheat releases natural sugar, and the starch in the flour turns to sugar, too.

A Taste of Spring

Haft mewah (hahft MEE-wah), a soupy fruit dish, is another sweet treat that is always served on Nauroz. Haft mewah is made of dried fruits and nuts that are served in their own syrup. Many different combinations

Senjed, a date-like fruit, are sometimes among the ingredients used in haft mewah, a sweet treat served on Nauroz, the Afghan new year.

Haft Mewah

Haft mewah is not difficult to make, but it must be refrigerated for a couple days. The longer the fruit soaks, the sweeter the juice becomes. Dried cherries, dried berries, walnuts, and/or yellow raisins can be substituted for any of the fruits or nuts. The nuts should be unsalted.

Ingredients

½ cup raisins
½ cup dried apricots
½ cup dates
½ cup prunes
½ cup figs
½ cup blanched, slivered almonds
4 cups cold water

Instructions

1. Combine all the ingredients in a large bowl. Cover the ingredients with water.
2. Cover the bowl with aluminum foil. Put the bowl in the refrigerator for two days.
3. Serve in bowls. Spoon the liquid over the fruit.

Serves 4.

can be used. Raisins, prunes, hazelnuts, pistachio nuts, walnuts, almonds, and senjed, a date-like fruit, are one popular mixture. The ingredients are soaked in water for at least two days. During this time, the dried fruits plump up and release natural sugar into the water, which turns to syrup. The way the fruit changes from dried and shriveled to plump and juicy symbolizes the start of spring to the Afghan people. Eating the sweet fruity dish is considered to be good luck. And, says author Sekandari, "It is very delicious and nutritious."[15]

Afghans eat haft mewah on March 21st, the first day of the New Year. Many Afghans stand in front of their home offering a spoonful of the sweet and the good luck associated with it to anyone who passes by.

Whether sharing haft mewah with passersby, spending the night at a samanak party, savoring halwa on Eid ul-fitr, or breaking the Ramadan fast with boulani, Afghans like to celebrate. Sharing special foods helps make every celebration more memorable and fun.

Metric Conversions

Mass (weight)

1 ounce (oz.)	= 28.0 grams (g)
8 ounces	= 227.0 grams
1 pound (lb.) or 16 ounces	= 0.45 kilograms (kg)
2.2 pounds	= 1.0 kilogram

Liquid Volume

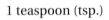

1 teaspoon (tsp.)	= 5.0 milliliters (ml)
1 tablespoon (tbsp.)	= 15.0 milliliters
1 fluid ounce (oz.)	= 30.0 milliliters
1 cup (c.)	= 240 milliliters
1 pint (pt.)	= 480 milliliters
1 quart (qt.)	= 0.96 liters (l)
1 gallon (gal.)	= 3.84 liters

Pan Sizes

8-inch cake pan	= 20 x 4-centimeter cake pan
9-inch cake pan	= 23 x 3.5-centimeter cake pan
11 x 7-inch baking pan	= 28 x 18-centimeter baking pan
13 x 9-inch baking pan	= 32.5 x 23-centimeter baking pan
9 x 5-inch loaf pan	= 23 x 13-centimeter loaf pan
2-quart casserole	= 2-liter casserole

Temperature

212°F	= 100°C (boiling point of water)
225°F	= 110°C
250°F	= 120°C
275°F	= 135°C
300°F	= 150°C
325°F	= 160°C
350°F	= 180°C
375°F	= 190°C
400°F	= 200°C

Length

¼ inch (in.)	= 0.6 centimeters (cm)
½ inch	= 1.25 centimeters
1 inch	= 2.5 centimeters

Notes

Chapter 1: A Cultural Connection

1. Helen Saberi, *Afghan Food & Cookery*. New York: Hippocrene Books, 2000, p. 46.

2. Humaira Ghilzai, Katie Morford, "Rice and Pasta, Palau: Afghanistan's Classic Rice Dish," Afghan Cooking Unveiled, April 7, 2010. www.afghancooking.net/afghan-cooking-unveiled/rice-pasta/.

3. Katie Morford, "Recipes: Yogurt the Crowning Touch for Afghan Recipes," Afghan Cooking Unveiled, February 6, 2010.

Chapter 2: An Honored Tradition

4. Quoted in Michael Yessis, "Q&A with Paul Kvinta: Travels with Rory Stewart in Afghanistan," World Hum, June 28, 2007. www.worldhum.com/travel-blog/item/paul_kvinta_on_rory_stewart_and_afghanistan_20070627/.

5. Nafisa Sekandari, *Afghan Cuisine Cooking for Life*. Bloomington, IN: First Books, 2003, p. 33.

6. Nafisa Sekandari, *Afghan Cuisine Cooking for Life*, p. 40.

7. Katie Morford, "Rice & Pasta—Afghan Dumplings with Spiced Lamb and Yogurt Sauce," Afghan Cooking Unveiled, April 3, 2010. www.afghancooking.net/afghan-cooking-unveiled/rice-pasta/.

Chapter 3: Tea and Snacks

8. Quoted in "Green Tea Morning," Afghanaid. www.afghanaid.org.uk/pages/green_tea_morning.html.

9. Helen Saberi, *Afghan Food & Cookery*, p. 270.

10. Jiffer Bourguignon, "Afghan Appetites," Saveur.com, November 2004. www.saveur.com/saveur-travels/europe-middle-east-and-asia/afghan-appetites-1000031104.html.

11. Quoted in Joanna Kakissis, "Jalalabad's Sweet Ice Cream Shop,"

World Hum, June 3, 2008. www.worldhum.com/travel-blog/item/jalalabads_sweet_ice_cream_shop_20080602/.

Chapter 4: Special Foods for Special Days

12. Quoted in Hind Al Yousef, "Only Traditional Food in Their Afghan Home," Gulf News, November 5, 2008. www.gulfnews.com/gulf/uae/heritage-culture/only-traditional-food-in-their-afghan-home.

13. Katie Morford, "Afghan Dessert That Is In A Category All Its Own," Afghan Cooking Unveiled, March 20, 2010. www.afghancooking.net/afghan-cooking-unveiled/sweets/.

14. Quoted in "Somonak—Afghanistan Womens Party," About-Afghanistan.com. www.about-afghanistan.com/afghanistan-womens-party.html.

15. Nafisa Sekandari, *Afghan Cuisine Cooking for Life*, p. 116.

Glossary

ashak: An Afghan dumpling filled with potatoes or green onions.

boulani: Stuffed fried bread.

chalau: White rice that is used in many Afghan dishes.

chapli kebabs: Grilled ground meat similar to hamburgers.

char marsala: Popular Afghan spice mix of cinnamon, cardamom, cumin, and cloves.

Dari: A language similar to Persian spoken in Afghanisan.

gandana: An Afghan vegetable similar to a green onion or leek.

haft mewah: A soupy fruit dish served for Nauroz.

halwa: A pudding-like sweet dish.

kebab: Afghan term for grilled, baked, or broiled meat.

korma: Thick sauce similar to stew that is served over rice.

legumes: Beans, lentils, and peas.

mast: Afghan yogurt.

mantu: A dumpling filled with meat.

marinates: To soak meat, poultry, or fish in sauce before cooking.

naan: Afghan word for bread.

Nauroz: Afghanistan's New Year's celebration.

palau: Cooked rice layered with meat and/or vegetables.

qabili palau: A mix of rice, lamb, spices, carrots, onions, and raisins that is Afghanistan's national dish.

Ramadan: A month-long religious holiday in which Muslims fast from dawn to dusk.

samanak: A wheat pudding eaten on Nauroz, and a female-only party in which the pudding is prepared.

Silk Road: Ancient connecting roads and trails that linked Asia to the Middle East and Europe.

tandoor: A beehive-shaped clay oven.

For Further Exploration

Books

Simon Adams, *Afghanistan*. London: Franklin Watts, 2009. Information about Afghanistan's history, geography, and issues currently facing the nation.

Sharifah Enayat Ali, *Afghanistan*. NY: Benchmark, 2006. Looks at Afghan history, geography, government, and culture with maps and color photos.

Tony O'Brien, *Afghan Dreams: Young Voices of Afghanistan*. NY: Bloomsbury, 2008. Afghan children talk to the author about their lives, and includes lots of photos.

Kathryn Pohl, *Afghanistan*. London: Franklin Watts, 2008. This colorful book focuses on daily life in Afghanistan.

Websites

Countries and Their Cultures, "Afghanis" (www.everyculture.com/wc/Afghanistan-to-Bosnia-Herzegovina/Afghanis.html). Information on Afghanistan's culture with recipes and links.

National Geographic Kids, "Afghanistan," (http://kids.nationalgeographic.com/kids/places/find/afghanistan/). Facts about Afghanistan's geography, history, climate, and culture with beautiful color photos.

Scholastic, "Kids in Afghanistan," (http://teacher. scholastic.com/scholasticnews/indepth/afghanistan_ kids/). Information about life in Afghanistan with a slide show and interviews with Afghan children.

Index

Picture credits

About the Author

Barbara Sheen is the author of more than 60 books for young people. She lives in New Mexico with her family. In her spare time, she likes to swim, garden, read, and walk. Of course, she loves to cook!